Jay Stays on the Job

by Carlos Ash
illustrated by Susan Lexa

Practice Decodable 62

McGraw Hill Education

Bothell, WA • Chicago, IL • Columbus, OH • New York, NY

MHEonline.com

Send all inquiries to:
McGraw-Hill Education
8787 Orion Place
Columbus, OH 43240

ISBN: 978-0-02-132866-6
MHID: 0-02-132866-8

Printed in the United States of America.

7 8 9 CTM 23

Every day, Jay brings mail.
Jay brings mail, rain or shine.

On hot days, you may stay in shade.
Jay walks in the hot sun's rays.

On gray, rainy days, Jay still brings mail.
Wet weather will not make him stay in.

On cold, cold days, you play inside.
Yet Jay remains on the job.

"I am paid to bring mail," explains Jay.
"Weather will not get in the way."

Did you get mail?

If you see Jay, say "Thanks!"